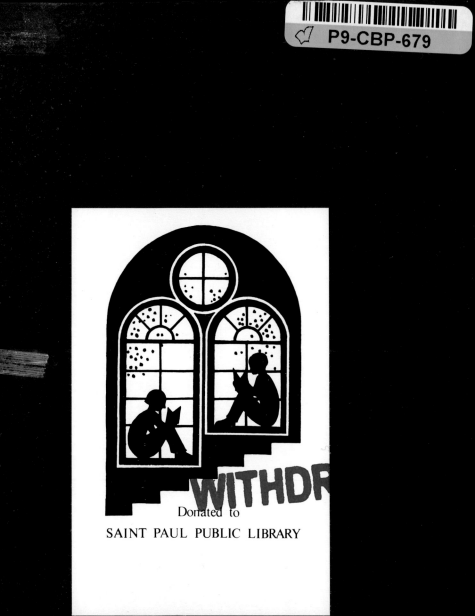

Flash Paper

Theresa Pappas

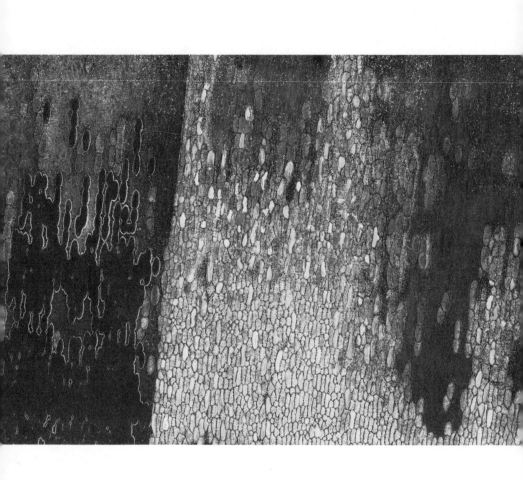

Flash Paper

Theresa Pappas

with graphics by
C. D. O'Hare

New Rivers Press 1985

Minnesota Voices Project Number 26

Copyright © 1986 by Theresa Pappas
Library of Congress Catalog Card Number: 85-62852
ISBN 0-89823-074-8
All rights reserved
Typesetting: Peregrine Cold Type
Book Design: Gaylord Schanilec
Author Photograph by Sam Pritchard

Some of these poems have appeared previously in the following publications: *Abraxas,*
The Akros Review, The Antioch Review, Calliope, Cedar Rock, Cottonwood, The Denver Quarterly,
GiltEdge, New Series, The Laurel Review, The Louisville Review, Mid-American Review, Painted
Bride Quarterly, Poet and Critic, and *Tar River Poetry.* Our thanks to the editors of these
publications for permission to reprint here. Special thanks to the MacDowell Colony,
where some of these poems were written.

Flash Paper has been published with the aid of grant support from the Jerome
Foundation, the First Bank System Foundation, the Arts Development Fund of the
United Arts Council, and the McKnight Foundation.

New Rivers Press books are distributed by

Bookslinger   and   Small Press Distribution
213 East 4th St.   1784 Shattuck Ave.
St. Paul, MN   Berkeley, CA
55101   94709

Flash Paper has been manufactured in the United States of America for New Rivers Press
(C. W. Truesdale, editor/publisher), 1602 Selby Ave., St. Paul, MN 55104 in a first
edition of 1,000 copies.

for Martone

Flash Paper

III. *Habits*

IV. *Nowhere Near*

SUNDAYS

On Sundays there was nothing
that wasn't foreign. God squinted
through the chandelier to where I stood
on the balcony, a blue-robed crowd
ascending the wall around him, his beard
tangled in clouds. Far below, the priest
swam in a thick light, lifting
his arms, swaying against
the altar, incense and his voice
spiralling. Everyone else spoke Greek and knew
when to stand or murmur together. I watched
God's eyes or swivelled to look
at the windows, those handsome
men, their stories unknown to me.

Afterwards at the bar, I played
pinball or, in the back room,
darts. My father's friends
were opaque. Their hair didn't float
around their heads. Bob, Jim, and Bernie
intoned their loud stories.
The long mirror gave back
the flat sheen of bottles, the glimmer
of eyes. When it got late, the women,
wrapped in a cosmetic aura, always
pushed their faces close to mine.
And I was afraid they would say something
essential as they spoke to me
in this solemn, other tongue.

BOOKIE

"He was surrounded by a golden glow,"
Mr. Metcalf told Judge Northrop.

— *Baltimore Sun*

You stand in the center
of the room, arm outstretched,

flourishing the sheet
of paper, still creased

from your pocket and buckling
in your fingers. You hold

one corner loosely,
and the paper crackles

as though already burning.
In your other hand, the lit

cigarette swerves, a turn
of the wrist, and the room fills

with light. You step back
and smile as the flames hang

for an instant and vanish
leaving an odor, but no ash.

There are other times you must
perform, surrounded by men

closing in on your columns
of numbers, but this display

is for your children, and the flash
paper you unfold for them is blank.

LESSONS

In the basement of the art store
the ladies learned to paint.
I was only ten and shy about joining them there
on Friday evenings while my brother
sat at the back of the music store
bent over his new guitar
and my father waited somewhere for our lessons to end.
Inside the art store, there were racks of books —
How to Draw Dogs, or hands, or barns,
or women. I was sure it was better to study
in class, with the teacher leaning at my shoulder.
Often she took the brush from my hand though,
and even at that age I was embarrassed
to call the finished paintings my own.
From other parts of the room I could hear
the ladies talking, bragging sometimes
about their children, girls I knew at school.
My family was proud of the paintings
and hung them in weathered frames the art store sold.
But when I looked at them, I saw
the eddying of my teacher's hand
across the board, daubs and flourishes
added to the stagnant patches I knew were mine.
The teacher said there was a way
to paint everything, certain twists
of the brush that would capture
the look of wet blossoms or faraway trees.
How to paint: sky (the blue layers
deepening as they approached
the top of the board); tarnished wood
on picturesque boats or sheds
or window frames; clouds, branches,
leaves, grass, fields, flowers; fur
of a cat; white tips of waves
and the gulls hanging over them.
I imagined thousands of manuals
like those upstairs, one for each thing

on earth. Laboring over a flat, sullen
corner of my board, knowing
the teacher could spill in light
and air with just a few brisk gestures,
I took comfort in the tools
I could not master. The handle
on my tidy wooden case curved in my palm
when I carried it. I unfastened
the metal clasps, set down the box,
and propped the lid to exhibit
the contents, as though *they* were the art:
the palette snug in its grooves,
the small golden oil jar, the metallic
tubes with their graphic names — *burnt*
and *raw* and *cobalt*, the slim knife,
and the regiment of brushes.
Holding these objects I believed
that when I found their secrets, they'd yield
to me as they did to my teacher.
I stared at the photograph or the postcard
clipped to my easel, yearning to secure
their stubborn forms. In that class
I never learned, I never learned to love
the things I painted — plaits of rope
looping from a nail, stone fence tumbled
beside an orchard, rectangle of pasture
through the window of an abandoned farmhouse.
I hoped someday I'd get so good
I wouldn't even have to look anymore.

PLAYING TIME

On the front steps, our mothers wait for us, flushed
in their pastels and bermuda shorts. Our jump
ropes have coiled to the ground, chalk margins dissolved
on the avenue. It's getting dark as we lean
back on their sunburned knees, while they talk as though
we aren't there about the note Irene left her
husband, the hole Jim put in the bedroom wall
with his fist, and how thirteen-year old Betty
teases her hair now. Then they teach us a game
called Time. The mothers nod and touch our shoulders
to tell us where to sit. They ask questions and
range us on the steps by our answers. Joy and
Janie answer, take new places, answer, brush
against me as they move again. The questions
are hard: I finally lose each step I gain.
The game can't end. We play Time for hours. I wait
for my turn and follow the croon of questions,
the signals to move, the mild halt of a wrong
answer, the penalty of descent. Passing
cars brighten the asphalt briefly, the rub of
tires erasing for a moment the sounds of
crickets and cars down on Belair Road. It's dark
now. I can't see the scoop of freckles on my
mother's neck, so I look through the trees for a
simple constellation, something I would know.
I listen for my own mother's voice. She speaks
tonight without the strain of calling me, as
she must each day to span the neighborhood with
the syllables of my name, calling me to
lunch and supper, chores and sleep, calling me away
from other games. This time I want to answer.

SATURDAYS AT THE PARAMOUNT

The Vikings blur and we become lost
in the tumult of smoke and waves.
My brother and I sit so close to the screen
we can't quite see the edges
where the lepers lean together
in embarrassed clusters. We have to move
our heads to follow the flash of weapons
surging toward a high, high wall,
and we strain back our necks to see the gods
looking down over everything and bickering
among themselves. Up close like this,
we can't be distracted by the chatter
and squirming of children in other rows.
Our tilted faces reflect
the mild glow that Jesus radiates.
(Why don't they show him?
we wonder.) The pharoah's shadow
stalks across our foreheads.
Sometimes my brother murmurs,
admiring the clean swipe of a blade
or the awfulness of an adversary.
Sometimes I close my eyes
and let the sound carry me along
with the huge upheavals of people
and weather, the two indistinct,
inseparable. Crowds roll across hills
while storms gather in the sky.
Men balance bows, drag oars,
heap boulders. Their garments look weighted.
They haul their bodies too.
They curse the heavens or they pray out loud,
caught in squalls of madness, ambition,
vengeance, faith. And the women, another kind
of weather, clothes pulled taut
against their own turbulence,
hair forged into elaborate helmets.
When Jason faces those skeletons

springing from the dirt, when the fishes
and loaves are handed round,
when pyramids rise — watching, we recognize
it all, the violence, the sweat, the divine.
Outside, on Belair Road, still Saturday
afternoon, the colors aren't as bright.
Even Woolworth's window across the street
seems faded and dim. The buses moan,
the cars bleat weakly. We hardly hear them.
We know that what we see
inside the Paramount is true, is history.
Long ago, our grandparents, perhaps
even our mother and father, abandoned
those embattled regions. Somehow
they learned to settle
for these daily rhythms:
faint but insistent as the sea
heard from a distance at night,
as the traffic heard from our apartment
blocks away. We follow the curbstones home,
knowing that we too will surrender.
We'll abdicate. We'll give up
our crowns, our shields, our halos.

OLYMPIA

"Heaven," you once asked,
"of what colors are you composed?
Why have you suddenly separated
me from my brothers
and sisters?" Remembering you only
white-haired, creaking
on the porch, barely able to speak
my language, your toothless
humor making me nervous, I now
collect pictures of the sturdy
beauty you used to be.

The mute year before death
when they stored you upstairs
with your icons, I avoided the slow
climb to the skyless room, trembling
hands and coins pressed
into my palm, your new language
even more foreign, your eyes
even moister with silence. I wish
you'd told me more, when you still
had a voice, about the boy you kissed
in the olive grove, the older
sister who refused
to marry, the distances you travelled.

IN AMERICA, GRANDMOTHER

... someone could not help
admiring the beauty of a
child.

— Lawrence DiStasi, *Mal Occhio: The Underside of Vision*

Your incense still haunts
the upstairs from this morning,
when we went to church but you stayed
here with your saints. Ashes cool
in the brass cup beneath the mild eyes
of those women. The hallway is steamy,
and my brother and I drift sleepily
from tub to pajamas you unfold
for us. Our skin is damp.
My hair clings to my neck, rivulets
of soapy water snaking down my back.

On the ride to church, we pass three cemeteries:
smudged walls and black fences along the sidewalk,
buckets of flowers at the gates, slow cars
rolling among the bright slabs and their shadows.
Our church is made of stones, and old women
who look like you touch my face and my brother's,
saying words above our heads in your language.

When you wrap us in towels, your hands
test our limbs: we are perfect, and
the sounds you now whisper might save us.
In bed, we watch lights from cars slip
through the blinds and wind across the walls.
What things breathe, we wonder, in the snugness
of closets, in the corners untouched by light?
We try to give them names before we fall asleep,
tucked in, in danger, at home
with you, Grandmother, in America.

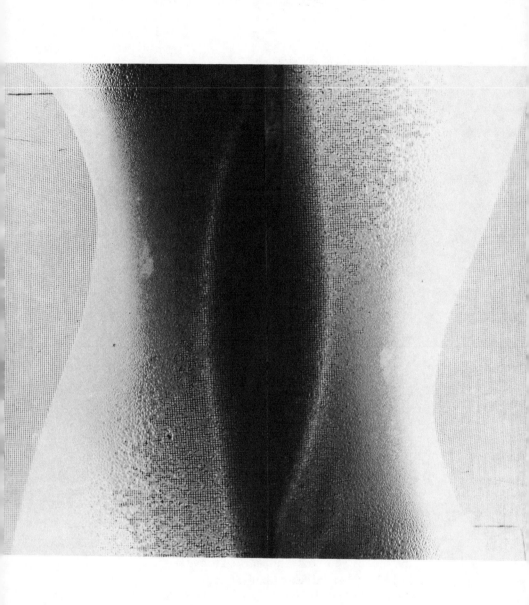

II. Guide to the Island

FIRST NIGHT IN ATHENS

1. Distant Cousins
I lift a spoonful of soup, and the old man whispers, *Bravo.*
His sister presses a napkin to her eyes and nudges
my plate towards me. There's too much furniture here.
We're surrounded by photographs: tight worried faces,
all watching me eat. My cousins trace my brow,
stroking my hair aside with unsteady hands,
and they take down one picture, a woman my age when she stood
before those waxy columns and trailing vines. They call
me by her name, *Olympia, Olympia,* the accent numbing
the third syllable. They call me *little girl*
and point toward the ceiling. I must lean back to see
inside the ornate frame, this photograph assembling
single portraits — the father's black-rimmed eyes
and thin lips shimmering above the mother's solid shoulder,
a daughter almost grown, two small children.
Each face smolders in a different light. These figures,
stitched together with ragged, ashen seams,
look bewildered, just wakened from sleep, or death,
not expecting to find us gathered here.
A fine silt drifts across them. My old cousins
pronounce the names of the things they touch — *bread,*
door, table, cup — and wait for me to make the sounds.

2. Luna Park
The old man leads me down to streets brighter
than the rooms we leave behind, sidewalks lit
by cars, kiosks on each corner. He tucks my hand
into the crook of his arm, keeping me at his side.
Cautious at the crossings, attentive as a sweetheart,
he stops at a kiosk to buy candy, while I stare
at the clotted headlines and wonder what has happened.
He unwraps the paper and foil, offers me the pastel
tablet I don't know how to refuse. *Good,* I say,
good, as I hold it on my tongue. We pass
through an archway, beneath huge, coiled letters,
and move along aisles of orbiting bulbs, machinery

hauling girls into the sky, children balancing
plumes of cotton candy. The old man walks slowly,
urging me to say words I should know. *Hair, ear, teeth, hand.*
My little girl, he says, gripping my fingers, pressing
into a crowd. He thinks I pull back because I'm afraid
of the ride. The cars rest heavily on the metal floor,
round noses pushed together. I remember, as a child,
how tightly I held the steering wheel and waited
for the jolting start, how the sparks sizzled above my head
as I hurtled toward another car. But here,
adults, solemn, peer from the other cars and drive
in a stately circle, hugging the wall.
Beside me the old man spins the tiny wheel
and waves at the sights beyond Luna Park. Our car lumbers
on like an overfed beast, tame and sad. I pretend
I'm a child. *Tree*, I say. *Beautiful. Lights.*
I pretend there's some reason I should join
this procession. Some reason I should be here at all.

NIGHT FISHING

The disc of light falters, tracking
the twist of hands in yellow
mesh. We sweep Parikia Bay for an hour
to find the marked nets, and now, past

midnight, Vasili speaks as he pulls.
There are two kinds of fish. The ones
we'll eat tomorrow flip into the blue
plastic that Maya raises, sleek

cylinders arcing from a deft release.
Urs holds the flashlight, follows their paths
from the net, and then returns the beam
to Vasili's hands. The other fish

Vasili calls scorpions, warning us
they are not to be eaten
as he works the fibres apart from barbed
edges. I am silent in the bow and watch

closely at first the intervals
of hauling between snags
of fish, the loosening, the drop
into the bag. The scorpion-fish

outnumber the others, and Vasili stops
talking, intent on the splintering
of their brittle fins. The air
begins to chill around me. I look

back to the cafes on shore.
Above the town, the hill's rim
melts and the moon erupts, egg-shaped,
balancing at the peak. Voices

cross the water. The moon
inserts itself onto the sky, flat
and full, sucking its glow
from the hill. I am tired

of this rocking, but the net still
slides into the boat, and Vasili's fingers,
slowing and drugged, must uncatch
each spiny poison fish.

GUIDE TO THE ISLAND

In the morning he leans at the sink
to bathe, to shake the dust from his lashes
and curls, to watch himself
in the mirror and let me watch him. He tries
on different faces and clothes, anticipating
the day ahead, the harsher light. On the table
by the bed he has left shreds of cellophane,
crackers, matches, and his knife.

"If women have minds, then I am an airplane
pilot," the waiter giggles, gesturing
at a table of tourists. I order
yogurt, bread, and coffee, while another
boat sails without me. The waiter
sets down his tray to outline the merits
of the Soviet Union. Lemon rinds and blue
plastic bags wash onto the rocks below the cafe.

Another stranger eyes me with extravagant
sorrow and seems surprised that I say no
to anything. He bares his gold teeth, happy
to talk about his soccer team, faithless
German girls, and what it means to be Greek
and a man. He fingers his cigarette, assuring
me he does not mind if he buys a girl
a coffee and it does not lead to bed.

At the Naxos Club, Saki spins the records
and lights, grinning from his alcove
at the dancers. Another Saki, finished
waiting tables down the beach, pushes
past the swinging door, flings his jacket
to a chair, steps onto the dance floor. One
more Saki, a thin black dog, sleeps near the bar,
breathing on the heels of the smudged woman there.

The Disco Rock throbs beneath Ariadne's
Gate, a temple begun in 523 B.C. but never
finished. Along the promenade I hear
voices from the cake shop, women
sharpening the edges of their language.
Thanassos approaches from a darker
shop where men are gathered. He presses
his room key into my hand and walks away.

LIKE SHELLS

there's a thirst there's a love
there's an ecstasy
all hard like shells
you can hold them in your palm

— George Seferis

"Do you do this — in America?"
Your body, taut against mine, hesitates,
but I won't answer. All night
in the club, I watched you.
You moved without lifting
your feet, shuffling at the edge
of the dance floor, or you took

the arms of your "brothers," snagging
time in the measured swoops
and turns. I think of the symmetry
of your two missing teeth, the gaps tucked
in the corners of your smile, the sweets
you buy for yourself, how you sit
on the bed dipping your knife

into a can of cherries, licking
the syrup, brown skin
against the sheet. In the morning, I follow
you along arched narrow
streets, shop to shop. You weigh
potatoes in your hand, gather
vegetables, bread, meat, quietly

bargaining to make
a meal for your friends who
lean to me, hinting at sadness, shaking
their dark heads: "You must
be good to him." In your room in the Hotel
Dionysos, I unfold your black
vinyl pants and the torn

31

sweater with the llama. I touch all
your clothes, everything frayed
and soft. Nothing fits you.
When we find a beach below the church
of Agia Ana, you leap
from rocks, launching
a towel to dam up the pools, to trap

the small fish. You kneel beside
my mat and uncap the sun
lotion. I start to say no, I see a boat
moored nearby, but you won't stop until I sleep
in the glare, my lips raw from the salt
of you, minute imprints of shells
fading from my skin.

CORFU

When I was still a boy,
I was afraid of my mother's rooms:
heavy women and furniture blotting out
the sun, shutters and curtains, tense
needlework of sisters, threads in Mama's hands,
the soup, the bread my father came home for.

I was afraid of his stare
and stiffness, like the ancestors
arranged on all the shelves and walls.
In one small photograph, my father,
still young, was smiling,
but I could tell that even then it meant nothing:

he knew how to control
the muscles of his face, how to fill
his uniform. When he turned to me,
I learned not to look at his eyes.
I saw the floor tilting away
and waited for his hands.

My mother was silent, a blur
of ritual motion, preparations not for me.
Outside I heard voices, words that weren't prayers,
and there were lights, but always when I came home,
my father's shadow behind the door seized away
the night, the street, the life.

HELLAS — SOUVENIR

The sky is deeper than those cluttered waves,
and nothing washes across it
but a few frail garlands of cloud.
Beneath that calm expanse, she is held
atop the water as though reclining on cushions.
White ruffles splash as she rocks ashore
along with the wreckage of a gaily painted boat —
orange and yellow and green.
No men aboard, its oarlocks gaping.
The mermaid's trident and the little broken prow
point ahead to a triangle of black sand.
The mermaid looks wearily at nothing,
streamers of copper light trailing
her heavy hair. Scales unfold
down her tailfin like a child's idea
of golden coins, the brightest yellow crayon.

I'm used to being cast about
by shifting currents. Not animal, not human,
not divine — I seem a little of each.
I loiter at the edges of those realms.
You see me only when you're terribly alone.
You've stared into the waves too long.
Your pockets have filled up with sand.
Then you see the serrated rock
against the sky. You see the empty boat.
You see me riding toward you on the tide.

WEST PEDIMENT, TEMPLE OF ZEUS, OLYMPIA

What's left of us still struggles. Caught
in fragments of each other's limbs.
Our faces altered by the silt
that washed across them. Some parts
never found. If just one hand
or a single brow remained. Even then
you'd see the battle that grips us all.

IN AGAMEMNON'S TOMB

The walls rise beside us
as we kick through the dust toward the entrance.
Inside, a young Greek tour guide lifts her passionate voice.
No human sacrifice, she says to the American retirees
surrounding her. Heads tipped back, they all stare upward
into the dark. *There was never any human sacrifice here,*
the woman insists, though no one disagrees.
The Americans listen politely.
They've seen enough of this hull of stone.
But their guide keeps shouting, her words becoming shrill:
No matter what you have heard

NECROMANTEION

The bus leaves the coast to cross
flat shards of farmland
pieced out against the pale sky.
A landscape like a train set: tidy cypress trees
put down on their small stands, an arch of polished water
irrigating each field.

Or like a bad painting: the world's not this neat,
the artist scratched in details
he couldn't possibly see, those blades of light
paring every seam.

Our guide's face has been erased (accident or fire?)
and drawn back in again, crudely. The planes between
his features vacant as the sky that chafes our window.
One eye a smudge, its lid dipping in permanent sorrow,
even when he laughs, which he does often —
leaning toward the driver, his skin shivers like pondwater
scored by an insect, the crease of mouth tightens.

Before we reach the site, he pitches down the aisle,
suddenly remembering his duties, waving little maps
with chambers labelled *alpha, beta,*
gamma, delta, arrows swerving through the maze
to the underground vault where people talked to the dead
and believed they heard the dead talk back.

Once there we see that the tops have sunken
from most of the rooms. The maze walls stand knee-high.
We don't need diagrams to find the opening in the ground
and the metal steps descending,
like the ones the school janitor took to the Boiler Room,
his footfalls echoing upward.

We think we'll hear something, down in this cool vault,
if only we remain still enough.
But our clothes whisper along our limbs,
and our pulses eddy around, drowning out the voices
the pilgrims came to hear.

Above in the glare, among the toppled rocks,
our guide tells the other tourists
about the priests' deceptions — the drugs,
the invisible devices — and all the money they collected.
He laughs again at the foolish, foolish pilgrims.
The dead aren't here, he says. *They never were.*
We know he's right, but we've come a long way.
We stay underground, wishing we could be tricked
into hearing them. Wanting at least to sense
the machinery locking into place. And behind the secret panel,
the priests whispering together before they answer
our questions, pretending to be the dead ones we must consult.

RIVER STYX

I won't get into the boat
because it has a motor.
That doesn't seem right —
too much noise
along that tranquil passage.

I'd rather sit beside the river
at this table, ordering small plates
of food and bottles of portokalada,
listening to the intimate buzz
of their language — bus driver,
tour guide, waiter.

When the others get back,
they say they went as far
as they could before the banks
narrowed and the reeds closed in around them.
"You should have gone," they keep saying,
but when I ask why, they won't answer.

WEDDING SONG

We don't know the language: still
we find a way to lie.
You mime the crossing of crowns
above our heads, and Anna — another old woman
in black, our landlady on this island — believes
we are married.

In her house we sleep beneath
a bamboo ceiling that creaks all night
as though alive, still tilting
in the wind somewhere.

Waking late, we hear the clack of looms
echoing from cool sheds. Brushes
scrub the pavement outside our door.
Children chant, choosing sides.

Soon we learn what to expect.
The children are called.
Niko plods over the hill with his donkey.
Anna enters the house carrying cloth just lifted
from her loom, repeating a word we now know,
work, work, tugging at her kerchief.

We walk the shuttered passages
at midday, seeing no one, careful
not to disturb the patterns of chairs
and tables when we sit in the empty square.
At the beach, we gaze out over the waves
as though waiting for something, or we fall asleep
in the sand as though giving up. Climbing
back to town, we nod to grandmothers in doorways,
to the hunched man who carves wooden forks and spoons.

Each day is the same, until one morning
we notice young girls raising strange bundles
in their arms and wonder what's folded in the ridges
of white cloth, why the girls look so smug as they press
along the streets in twos and threes.
Back at our rooms we find a saucer of pastries
steeped in honey. A wedding, Anna explains,
passing the phantom crowns through the air.

And later, drawing us across dark rooms
to the balcony, she sweeps her arm
toward the cliff above and one house brighter
than all the others. Beneath those radiant windows,
people gather, filling the narrow street.
When their voices swell around us on the breeze,
Anna says a word that must mean *song*.

One hand curved at her ear, one hand caught
against the black dress, above her heart —
she sways in the resonant night, wanting to tell us more.

III. *Habits*

FIVE PICTURE POSTCARDS

1. Florida's World Famous Weeki Wachi, Spring of Live Mermaids

It's not easy to smile
underwater, to keep
from squinting, to hold

these poses. That's why
our faces seem strained
and taut, our arching backs

unnatural. We try
to look at home
in the wrong element

as we kneel on the sandy floor
or languish against a rock,
even though we can feel

our lipstick dissolving
into the gauzy currents.
Fish nudge our fluorescent

swimsuits. Our breasts
rise in the tide.
You may think we're counting

seconds. You see the air
hose trailing away
behind us, the rush of bubbles

drifting upwards
with our clouded hair.
You see the castle

planted in the sand,
the green minaret,
the small dark doorways.

You don't believe this illusion
any more than we do.
But you want us to remain

submerged and smiling.
You want to keep looking at us
through blue veils of water.

2. Sleeping Muse: Brancusi

Along this pale gray
plane, I cool my lunar
cheek, my surfaces all
composed and gathered,
a cupful of darkness
pooled on the ledge
of marble brow.
Heavy as I am,
when you regard me
you think of hollow
eggshell, of empty hull:
a still enclosure
you would not want
to enter, it is enough
just to behold.
The sealed eyelids,
the narrow nose stem,
the damp blossom
of pressed lips:
these features
could erode even more,
they could wear away
under the weight
of your gaze.
But even then
you would recognize
the dreaming spaces
that I shelter here.

3. Nike Untying Her Sandal

The cloth caught against my skin
looks tangled, sticky, web-like.
It bunches and gathers along
my thighs, over my shoulder,
inside my elbow. It trails
in heaps behind me, heavier
and more unruly than my wings.
And yet, in all that fabric,
my form is not disguised:

instead it ripens within
these weighted veils.
This awkward, stooping pose
only reveals the grace that guards me.
Balanced on one foot, fussing
with the sandal strap of the other,
I am as regal as if already rising
into the sky, my wings unfurled,
clothing fluttering to earth.

4. Marble Cycladic Figurine
(2200-2000 B.C.)

Across this vast body
my features surface
like islands — the ridge
of nose and its thin shadow,
the neck slab that props
my flattened face,
the tapering breasts,
and the faint triangle
engraved above my thighs.
My arms enfold me, an equator.
My ankles meet, bound
together in stone.
No mouth, no eyes. I balance
upright on the curved
rims of my feet, waiting
for the chisel's intercession,
waiting to be completed,
or destroyed.

5. The Minor Goddess of the Snakes

I'm clay. My skirts fan
out in heavy slabs

to the hoop of dirt
they hug. Above

my narrow waist
the rest of my body

climbs, cinched to earth
by the strata of my gown.

These snakes aloft
in my fists would drag

me higher. They point
a swerving passage

toward the sky. But
there is a symmetry

that must be kept,
the fixed stare

of my breasts, my eyes:
I'm clay, yet I ache to rise.

BEATRICE REFLECTS

These poems are based on a brief *Life Magazine* article from the early 50's about a woman named Beatrice Turner, who lived during the first half of this century. When she was 17 years old, her parents withdrew her from art school because they objected to her seeing nude models. She spent the rest of her life at home, where she painted over a thousand self-portraits. When her father died, she kept his body around for two weeks while she painted his portrait. Beatrice's last drawings, before her death of malnutrition, were nude sketches of herself.

1. Life Drawing

The first time she removed
her kimono, I was shocked at the fact
of her flesh; until then I had only known
my own and never in such direct
light. I noticed the draughts
from the high studio windows and the stiff
pleats of my smock crossing
my chest. The model was my age
but she was swollen and almost as chalky
as the plaster casts mounted
on the walls. After weeks of still
lifes assembled by the instructor as he scolded
us about seeing, I didn't know where
to look. I was used to the open
mouths of jars, the terrain of crumpled
paper, austerity of chairs.

It was through the long poses
that I detected sinew, after she arranged
herself upon draperies, steadying
her feet or leaning on an elbow.
The instructor stood beside
the dais and cupped his hands
in the air around her, telling us
to squint, disclosing principles of life
drawing. As the minutes passed, color
pooled in splotches on her skin. I felt
I could trace the movement
of her blood. I began to see
things about her that could not be
drawn, and on my page her posture
hardened, her breasts did not pull
down. I tried to learn where she fixed
her eyes, what it was she watched
when she left us her body.

2. Daddy in Death

Stark against the cushion's floral pattern,
he leans, his surfaces reflecting
because of the black he wears
and Mother's scrubbing. The planes of his hair gleam
near the part, and his mustache hooks
the air. My eyes burn from the stillness
he secretes.

There's something fallen
about his brow, which sinks into a dreaming gaze.
Beside his ear, a pink spray blooms, a wreath
curves on the fabric near his arm. He would never
have chosen this chair, and he never sat for me,
but Mother propped him up, so I prepare
my paints.

3. Mother and Vase

It is her edges I want to get,
the profile, the curve of spine
above her dress. I've painted Mother many times,
though not as often as I've painted myself.
She is impatient with posing, she falls asleep.
I always paint her turning away, tilting
into a corner of the canvas.

Her contours would dissolve in fullness
if she faced me instead of the dark objects
that define her: feathers of a broad fan, its tendrils
twisting away from her pale skin,
and the vase handle that swells like a black fountain
around her head, crowding her aside.

On the body of the vase, a naked boy lifts
his arm, blessing or warning other figures obscured
by drifting tunics. A cherub sails
toward Mother's shoulder. She holds her neck
and back erect, but seems to sway beneath a weight.
Her features slacken under the coils of hair.

Her eyelids drop. She raises the fan between
herself and the vase, draws up
part of her gown loosely in her fingers.
She doesn't see the boy's gesture, the blurred
story on the vase. I trace the tension
along her arms before it slips away.

4. Self-portrait with Mother

Mother and I stand back
to back, the single left strap

of my gown reflecting the one
on her right shoulder. I stare

out from the foreground,
while she looks down, fading

behind me. These days she drifts
into recesses, objects dropping

from her hands. She is drawn
to windows, not for the view,

but for the glow she allows
through her lowered lashes

when she parts the curtain.

5. Final Sketches

Landscape does not intrude here. I do not yield
surface to what should remain
background: roads that only taper to smoke
along the horizon, hills mantling
their true shapes beneath foliage, endless
mutation of clouds unveiling
nothing. "Paint me a picture
of yourself," Daddy said. I've covered

hundreds of canvases, stretched
one painting over another. For every pose,
I wore the dresses Daddy liked, fabrics
Mother chose and pinned around me as I balanced
on a chair. I had the time
for adjustments, to perfect the symmetry
of my eyebrows and my skin's translucent
sheen, to practice the placement
of fresh flowers or a sash. I costume myself

to leave the house: a hat, a fur
and gloves, the veneer I compose
against the ones who call me a designing
female, guarding their sons. The Historical
Society refuses the paintings I donate. Neighbors
stare at my old-fashioned clothes, which I shed
at home now because they conceal the wash
that age applied to me. Each day I undress

for mirrors and try to delineate
what I've become. I let velvet, ermine,
and feathers fall to the floor. I no longer need
to eat and still my figure blooms
across pages, reclining in light. My heavy brushes
steep in a jar of oil during this delicate scrutiny,
these preliminary sketches, and I'm afraid
I may never finish this work
if my body continues its revelation.

HANSEL

Watching your back
as you struggle to build a fire,
your voice a steady chant against shadows,
I know what you fear and what you mean to protect.

You would rather be safe and starving at home
where the sounds of Father chopping wood
and Mother complaining fill your ears,
where you can stride around pretending to be older,
outside helping Father, free of skirts,
too busy to look at me.

Now that your trails out of here have vanished
and your small voice and fire won't stop the night
I wait for you to turn around
and recognize in me: yourself, this forest, the witch.

THE RED SHOES

I confessed. The ax fell and released me
to the static earth. I watched the shoes skip
into the forest with my feet, saw streams
of my blood twisting bright as the polished
leather. The glow through my lids drained into
night before I opened my eyes again.
I kissed the hand that held the ax and turned
slowly back to town and the church of men.

Their God became mine. I learned to prefer
absence of color, the mercy of blank.
It's easier to kneel while I rehearse
psalms of the guilty, repenting the dance.
Forgive my sin, that crimson wish. The priest
welcomes me in with my plain wooden feet.

THE GIRL WHO TROD ON A LOAF

Mother, when I was small and tore wings
from flies, it was to learn about pain,
to see if other creatures felt any more
than you did. I left ladybugs spitted

on the sewing needles in your basket
to surpise you. They waved their legs
awhile and then congealed, reminding me
of your mending lessons, the snarls

of that economical thread in my fingers.
Nothing was ever wasted in our house,
not a gesture. I hated your apron
because of the gravity of your hands

when they dragged against it, showing me
how good people bury themselves.
I wouldn't bow my head in church, like you
bending over the sticks you gathered,

never enough to keep us warm.
I went underground in my own way, sinking
through the mud on my stepping stone
of bread, crumbs I should have brought to you.

I balance on this pedestal, hearing voices
from above, my story sung to children falling
asleep in their beds, while wingless
flies and your tears crawl my skin.

THE TINDER BOX

The wedding took place in a week, and the dogs
all had seats at the table, where they sat
staring with all their eyes.
— Hans Christian Andersen

And they never blink. All three of them
sit around taking in everything
with those eyes-as-big-as, annoying me
with their dumb, relentless obedience.
They're not dumb, of course. They can talk,
but they say nothing to me — only to my husband,
the soldier, now King: "What does my lord command?"
Then they trudge off, toenails clicking importantly
along the halls, to get whatever it is he wants,
just as they came for me those nights.

My soldier. Back then I believed
he was a lovely dream. I stretched out
on the animal's back and let
the soldier look at me — that's all
he did the first night. Even that was forbidden.
The second night he came very close
and put his hands on my clothes.
I'd had such dreams before.
On the third night, I breathed in
his warm breath and watched through my lashes
when his reverent kisses began.

Mother and Father taught me how much
their Princess was worth: they kept me
in a copper tower, shielded from prophesy
and the pilfering eyes of common folk.
At breakfast they made me recount
my dreams: they knew where danger lay.
I waited to be stolen. Now they are dead.
Now I belong to the man I dreamed.

The dogs bring him gold, girls,
kingdoms — the obvious things, the things
he knows how to demand.
But I watch over a place they'll never find.
I still like to feel this soldier's hands
on me: their heat, the way they search
for what I refuse to surrender
with my beauty. From the cool frontier
of dreams, I stare back into his eyes.
Men honor what they cannot own.

HABITS

In a town where everyone is mad, it is
not good to be alone sane, and by reason
of its not being good it is not advisable.

— Aloysia Sigaea

The old woman on the corner likes my hat. All winter
I've seen her struggling up streets in her black
coat. She always wears a hat herself and would carry
a shoulder bag like mine, but her shoulder
slopes, "a slight defect," she tells me.

Plants sway from the high ceiling
of my room, growing wildly, defying
my neglect. The red flannel curtain
tempers the light. There are closets
filled with clothes I never wear
because I'm not ready yet. They've all
been carefully chosen and aren't meant
to be worn without certain preparations.

Julian writes love letters to Alexander and indulges
in his own madness. Alexander seduces girls with foreign
names. In the bar, he wears a pajama top patterned
with red and black diamonds. He giggles and imitates
Julian's gestures. He smiles slyly and says
"I'm twenty-three, *very* young, and *very* virile."

Sometimes I'm scared there is no space
between things or space itself
is material. Names dissolve
and I don't know what separates
me from the chair. I must learn
more names, how things fit: hierarchies,
styles, species, the particular
tree, the disease, and boundaries.

The boy in leather leans against someone else's red
car, looking bored. He sheds his jacket, shakes
his hair out of his face, and lights a cigarette. He shifts
his weight from his left foot to his right, dragging
his boot back and forth in the gravel. He drums the side
of the car with his long fingers. He shifts his weight
again. He pushes his fingers through his hair, resting
his hand briefly on the back of his neck.

A force works against me whenever I try
to say *always* or *never*. The dull pains
behind my eyes only started
after I said, "I never get headaches."
I'm not strong enough for complete
costumes yet. Instead of defining
me, they close in and I become
even less visible. I tie belts,
bracelets, scarves on one at a time
to get used to their power.

The hat is like the ones Mouseketeers
wore, but instead of sprouting ears, it has a yellow
plastic duck bill for a brim. Jane is the name stitched
in yarn on her hat, but I call her the Donald Duck Lady.
On summer mornings she waits for the bus
to Old Orchard Beach. Spikes of black
hair dart around damp eyes and cracking
patches of rouge. Her shopping bags pull her over
so the back of her neck swells from her cotton
shift, and she puffs and mumbles to her toes
in sandals. She looks up, surprised, at Congress Square.
She nods and blushes under the bill of her hat.

I've walked into a room of people
I don't know, people turning to see
who's walking by. I've found a table
and occupied it, throwing barriers
around me, daring anyone to step within
this circle of empty chairs, this book
tilted to ward them off. This is not
the perfect disguise. The wig's metal
combs dig into my scalp, the earrings clamp
relentlessly. When I move, the clasp
of my necklace scratches and the dress
chafes my armpits. My body still resists
the authority of what it wears. I must
make more alterations, not only
in the clothing, but in myself.

Charles sells his poems from a bench in front
of the library, and when he's not there, he sits
at a booth in the Candy Kitchen with papers spread
all around him. His shoes are too long, his clothes
are army green, and his poems are bad, but he says
he'd have another breakdown if he went back to work.
A young woman asks, "Don't you feel guilty
living off the government, taking food away from people
who really need it?" He blinks slowly: "I really
need it." She badgers him until he says, "Don't you
feel guilty being fat and consuming extra food
while people are starving?"

I have carried home bolts,
cut and pinned patterns,
learned from a tailor
how to match seams.
On hangers, dress whisper.
I have measured each hem,
knelt among yard goods,
bending myself to this work.
The costumes are ready.
Accessories glitter.
Inside the bureau,
fabrics are weaving.
Open the closet.
Fasten the narrow collar.
Fasten the buckles, fasten the cuffs.

Reverend Buck stands while the bus moves, so he can flirt.
He wears a Stetson and a string tie, and he croons
old melodies for the ladies, while his friend Sammy mutters
that he isn't really a man of the cloth. The woman
with starched hair vows that she won't have hanging
plants because spiders might drop onto her head. "My god,
you look nice, lady!" the Reverend shouts.

I cross town silently, testing
the ground through soft-soled shoes. I found
a new hat at Goodwill today. It closes
tight around my head and the wide brim frames
my vision. A scarf catches the sounds
vibrating in my throat. A belt tells
me I'm breathing. Bracelets and rings
help me make a fist. Eye-shadow
is good for staring. People are starting
to see me.

IV. Nowhere Near

SENTINELS

The way he unpacked and rolled
his tobacco at dusk,
I thought it was his smoking
that drew down the darkness.
It seemed his ritual breath
released each gesture of night
that smudged first his corner
of the room and finally dimmed
the printed curtains
at the farthest window.

I looked past these at how the sheets
drying outside hung rigid as sentinels
in the static air, tenting the yard
in a flat light. I pinned
them there, knowing they'd be visible,
even as this man moved close
to me, and even when I closed my eyes.

SKELETON KEY

You were on your way somewhere
when you stood still and shuttled
the key from palm to palm
as if you'd forgotten
what it might unlock.
I looked up from my work
to watch your dazed signals
across the living room.
Sometimes in bed beside you,
I want to repeat your name,
quietly, not to wake you,
but so you'll turn and touch me.
While you swayed in your trance
in the center of the rug,
I thought of what was locked
inside our house.
What do you want? I wondered.
Doesn't everything open
under your dreaming hands?

PRIVATE ENTRANCE

Sometimes visitors tilt in the doorway
and squint through the screen
as though in a fog. They call our names
in childlike voices, hands cupped
around their eyes until they sift out
my form stirring in the gray room.
I let them in slowly, evading the festive
currents they sweep inside. *Look
at all you've done,* they say, tugging
at the shades for light. My husband
moves his mouth into a smile.
Only I detect the scent like polished
wood that eddies up when he stands.
Oh, I want to tell him,
I love the sound of the metal
latch sliding into place
and the way it rattles in real weather.

TROMPE LE DEVINEUR

LOVERS — the first word we see along
the ledge of signs. Then GUY LOMBARDO
looming even larger. A black handprint

pools in the corner of another panel,
the fingers waving like underwater plants:
MONTREZ-MOI VOTRE MAIN. Painted messages

lurch across the boards in both French
and English. They draw us nearer to the guesser
who sits on his hanging scale, dragging

his feet and bobbing beneath the arrow
that sweeps a span of numbers. Families
push around in their brilliant clothes,

children damp and gritty from the beach.
At our backs, the bumper cars thud
and spark. The guesser slowly unwraps

a sandwich from a sheet of waxed paper.
Closer to the signs, we read the smaller
words wedged among squat question marks, liquid

numbers, and fractured hearts. What is our weight?
What car do we drive? We can pay the guesser
to tell us what we already know. When

did we meet? And what words did you say to me
another summer, years ago? The guesser squints
at us and chews. We stare at snapshots

and newsprint warping under glass, celebrities
posing against this arcade wall, the guesser
gray and small beside them. It's hard to believe

but the famous have stood here too — Donny and Bobby
and Bobby and Bobby and Frank. Their names spill
down the largest sign. Perhaps they fell

silent before this cardboard box as they sorted
through the litter of prizes: dull
buttons sewn to cards; envelopes of flattened

hairnets; broken candles; rubber bands.
We can hear the ocean fizzing blocks away.
When the guesser guesses wrong and wrong again,

we walk off with our secrets and our prize.

NOWHERE NEAR

The tea tastes green; steam glosses
my skin. I wrap the cup in my hands, turning
it slightly to warm each finger,
nodding to the heat, converting the light
through my lashes. I am nowhere near that
earth, damp, studded with leaves,
needles, the black stones sinking
under our shoes on the way to that hill
where the tree trunks hang back,
but the high branches arch toward us and make
sharp noises as the sun breaks
and breaks across our bodies. It is as though
I have no body now except when
tented in this mist, taking tea, or in a dream
like the one this afternoon:
I was nothing but a body, that someone
touched through clothing.

LETTER

From the seventh floor of the Poagston Arms,
you write that it rains every day.
Above the used car lot, flags hang
at half-mast. Ashes spray out of the incinerator
as you look across the street into the windows
of the terminal ward and watch nurses
make their rounds, room to room. You see
bodies wheeled away on carts.

Things are missing, you say, as you set
your belongings out on the mossy rug.
You find postcards I sent you years ago,
just like the ones I send now, the same
eager words. The squat clock-radio only receives
the mournful bleats of a country station.
At mail time, other tenants emerge from rooms,
old women with names like Bea and Viola and Pearl.

Shaved heads inscribed with scars, the brain
doctor's patients appear in the lobby. Veterans
post signs about America's lost. Passing trains
make the whole building tremble. A friend from high school
calls to list adulteries, divorces.
On television the president explains the war. You watch
late movies. Each time you look out, the hospital
facade seems heavier in the wet slanted light.

How changed all these things will be
when I'm there with you.

WET

I would write about you wet, you say.
It's been raining for days here too.
Inside, the fire sounds like damp laundry
warping on the wind. The light sinks
through clouds. Tree trunks blacken.
the rain stutters on the slick, caramel leaves
smearing the ground. Pine needles etch
the mud beneath my boots and gather like rust
along edges. The thick air enters everything.

At the pond, small creatures pulse
through greenish water, their movements
veiled, like mine in these drizzling woods.
There's a film I'd like to brush away
just to see it rush back in again: a sweep
of my hand, an instant of clarity, and then
the drops sliding down. The things I reach for
melt and slip, ebb and rise.
When we're together again, I'll come
toward you through the steam of my shower,
trembling beads caught along the spots
you most want to touch. Your hand will clear
some surface briefly for your kiss.

MAIN STREET

Before I came to live with you, I read
about the swampy ground the town was built on,
the passenger trains that used to stop —

"20 chances to leave every 24 hours."
The guide book even showed, in black and white,
the post office mural, The Evolution of Corn,

squat Mayan god to microscope. My family wonders where
I've gone — Idaho? Ohio? Night after night
I take this walk with you, tracing the usual route.

We've learned the limits of this town.
We know what we will find. White clouds
from the power plant drift over the life-size cow

that hangs at one end of Main Street.
In the hobby store, a dinosaur's tail
lashes through the broken glass case,

trains gather along the mesh of tracks,
a helicopter turns slowly on a string.
We pause at every window, aware of the slightest

changes, noting what stays the same:
cowboy hats, shoes, lacquered portraits of Jesus,
potholders shaped like vegetables.

Tiny, stiff dresses stand up on their ruffles.
Small overalls slouch beside them.
Most people here never walk the length

of Main Street, down one side and up
the other. Their cars rush by as if there
were someplace to go, roaring along

between stop signs. Sometimes we see boys
issuing from bars, faces pale against the savage
school colors. We read the messages

on their clothes. One night a girl leaned
her head against a wall outside the Whiskey River
and cried, washed in the beams of a car's headlights.

Once a man with a foreign accent asked us questions
about the town's power supply. We watch the lengthening
cobs the banker sets on his sill, the dates

on neat labels. We examine the patterns
chosen by brides. We look at the old depot,
now used for offices, and wonder

what it was like with all those chances
to go. You recite the names of trains until
a freight drowns out your voice and we sway

together beside the drumming wheels, prepared
for the stillness this passage will leave behind,
finding things to love, loving what remains.